Round Towers
of
Ireland

Christiaan Corlett is an archaeologist with the National Monuments Service of the Department of Housing, Local Government and Heritage. He has written, compiled and edited many books on subjects ranging from archaeology, history and folklore to early photography. His books include: *Glendalough, Antiquities of West Mayo, Jane W. Shackleton's Ireland* and *Inscribing the Landscape: the Rock Art of South Leinster*. Chris is also one of Ireland's leading photographers of archaeological and historical monuments, and the majority of the photographs in this book are his own work.

First published 2025 by The O'Brien Press Ltd., 12 Terenure Road East, Rathgar, Dublin 6, Ireland.
Tel: +353 1 4923333; Fax: +353 1 4922777; E-mail: books@obrien.ie. Website: obrien.ie
The O'Brien Press is a member of Publishing Ireland.

ISBN: 978-1-78849-516-5

Copyright for text and photographs © Christiaan Corlett 2025
The moral rights of the author have been asserted.
Copyright for typesetting, layout, design © The O'Brien Press Ltd.
Cover and inside design by Emma Byrne.
Map artwork by Anú Design, www.anu-design.com

All rights reserved. No part of this publication may be reproduced or utilised in any form or by any means, electronic or mechanical, including for text and data mining, training artificial intelligence systems, photocopying, recording or in any information storage and retrieval system, without permission in writing from the publisher.

8 7 6 5 4 3 2 1
29 28 27 26 25

Photography by Christiaan Corlett.
Other photography: The author and publisher thank the following for permission to use photographs and illustrative material: author photograph, Jane Meehan; p.9 (top, left) courtesy of the Royal Society of Antiquaries of Ireland; p.46 (bottom left) Trinity College Dublin. If any involuntary infringement of copyright has occurred, sincere apologies are offered, and the owners of such copyright are requested to contact the publisher.

Printed and bound by Drukarnia Skleniarz, Poland.
The paper in this book is produced using pulp from managed forests.

ROUND TOWERS
of
IRELAND

CHRISTIAAN CORLETT

THE O'BRIEN PRESS
DUBLIN

Round Towers of Ireland

#	Name	#	Name	#	Name	#	Name	#	Name
1	Aghagower	9	Clonmacnoise	16	Drumcliffe	24	Kells	33	Old Kilcullen	42	Swords
2	Aghaviller	10	Cloyne	17	Drumlane	25	Kilbennan	34	Oughterard	43	Taghadoe
3	Antrim	11	Devenish	18	Dysert Aenghusa	26	Killala	35	Rattoo	44	Timahoe
4	Ardmore	12	Donaghmore	19	Dysert O'Dea	27	Kilmacduagh	36	Rock of Cashel	45	Tullaherin
5	Armoy	13	Dromiskin	20	Glendalough	28	Kilree	37	Roscam	46	Turlough
6	Castledermot	14	Drumbo	21	Grangefertagh	29	Kinneigh	38	Roscrea		
7	Clondalkin	15	Drumcliff	22	Inis Cealtra	30	Lusk	39	Saint Brigid's Cathedral		
8	Clones			23	Inishkeen	31	Meelick	40	Saint Canice's Cathedral		
						32	Monasterboice	41	Scattery Island		

CONTENTS

INTRODUCTION 7

MIDLANDS 13
Rock of Cashel, Co. Tipperary 13
Roscrea, Co. Tipperary 16
Clonmacnoise, Co. Offaly 17
Timahoe, Co. Laois 20
St Canice's Cathedral, Kilkenny 22
Grangefertagh, Co. Kilkenny 23
Tullaherin, Co. Kilkenny 25
Kilree, Co. Kilkenny 26
Aghaviller, Co. Kilkenny 27

EAST 28
Clondalkin, Co. Dublin 28
Lusk, Co. Dublin 29
Swords, Co. Dublin 30
Glendalough, Co. Wicklow 32
Taghadoe, Co. Kildare 34
Castledermot, Co. Kildare 35
Old Kilcullen, Co. Kildare 37
St Brigid's Cathedral, Kildare 38
Oughterard, Co. Kildare 40
Dromiskin, Co. Louth 41
Monasterboice, Co. Louth 42
Donaghmore, Co. Meath 44
Kells, Co. Meath 46

SOUTH 48
Ardmore, Co. Waterford 48
Cloyne, Co. Cork 50
Kinneigh, Co. Cork 51
Rattoo, Co. Kerry 52
Dysert Aenghusa, Co. Limerick 53

WEST 55
Inis Cealtra, Co. Clare 55
Scattery Island, Co. Clare 57
Drumcliffe, Co. Clare 58
Dysert O'Dea, Co. Clare 59
Kilmacduagh, Co. Galway 61
Kilbennan, Co. Galway 62
Roscam, Co. Galway 63
Killala, Co. Mayo 64
Aghagower, Co. Mayo 66
Meelick, Co. Mayo 67
Turlough, Co. Mayo 69
Drumcliff, Co. Sligo 70

NORTH 72
Antrim, Co. Antrim 72
Armoy, Co. Antrim 73
Drumbo, Co. Down 74
Drumlane, Co. Cavan 75
Clones, Co. Monaghan 76
Inishkeen, Co. Monaghan 78
Devenish, Co. Fermanagh 79

Scattery Island round tower in the Shannon estuary, Co. Clare.

INTRODUCTION

Round towers have become a national icon in Ireland. They are the most prominent building on many early Irish ecclesiastical sites. Around seventy round towers, or partial remains of towers, are scattered around Ireland. There were many more that have disappeared. For centuries their distinctive form has fascinated all who have gazed up at them.

Historians and scholars have debated their purpose. They were viewed as ecclesiastical structures, but theories also abounded as to whether they were tombs, temples, observatories, refuges from raiders, treasuries or only belfries.

Round towers were designed primarily as bell-towers and were attached to some of the most prestigious churches in Ireland during the 11th and 12th centuries. In thickly forested and remote landscapes they announced the location of their nearby churches. From the top

Bell-towers were a feature of early medieval churches throughout Europe. Irish round towers are unusual in that these slender, tapered structures stand alone, separated from their associated church buildings. They would have invoked a sense of wonderment, reaching as they did to the heavens.

windows the bell would have rung out over quite a distance.

A few similar examples can be found in Scotland, namely at Brechin in Angus and at Abernethy, Perthshire, and there is a round tower to be seen at Peel Harbour on St Patrick's Isle, off the west coast of the Isle of Man.

In the early 19th century, when Irish was still widely spoken, people who lived in the shadows of these towers knew them as *cloictheach* (literally 'bell-house'). This was also the term used in the medieval Irish annals, compiled by monastic scribes to document historical events. But this did not stop historians coming up with fanciful explanations.

One theory suggested round towers were built by the Vikings to watch over the local Irish. Ironically, it was also suggested that they were built by the Irish churches to look out for Viking raids. Both explanations are false, but not nearly as improbable as the theories that emerged at the end of the 18th century that they were Druidic, Buddhist or Phoenician temples.

In 1845 antiquarian and archaeologist George Petrie published an essay that examined these towers within their early Christian church context. Using historical sources and architectural evidence, he demonstrated that they were bell-towers and were constructed prior to the arrival of the Anglo-Normans in Ireland in 1167. He also suggested that the towers were used as places for refuge from attack as well as places to store church valuables, including relics and holy books. One theory he dismissed was that they may have been designed to house hermits. Ireland's earliest saints were known to take a prolonged period of reclusive prayer before founding a monastery. This theory is worth reconsidering, but there remains a lot about these monuments that we do not understand. Several towers are found at churches that were important places of pilgrimage, such as Glendalough and Inis Cealtra, and they may have acted like beacons to pilgrims on the final leg of their spiritual journey.

Engraving of the round tower at Clonmacnoise, Co. Offaly, based on a drawing by George Petrie and published in his 1845 *The Ecclesiastical architecture of Ireland anterior to the Anglo-Norman invasion, comprising an essay on the origin and uses of the Round Towers of Ireland.*

Above left: When the Office of Public Works reconstructed the roof of the round tower at Glendalough in 1876 they used a wooden scaffolding that closely resembled the method used by the original masons to build the tower nearly 800 years earlier.

Above right: The elevated doorway and tapered shape of the round tower at Ardmore, Co. Waterford.

Above left: Looking up the round tower at Timahoe, Co. Laois. The former timber floors were supported on offsets, where the inner face wall was set back to create narrow ledges.

Above right: At Aghagower, Co. Mayo, rings of projecting stones or corbels once supported the wooden floors. Inside the tower are the remains of plaster, which may indicate the walls were painted.

Above left: Whitewashed walls and reconstructed wooden floor within the round tower at Dysert Aenghusa, near Croom, Co. Limerick.
Above right: The conical roof and the bell-floor at the top of the round tower at Turlough, Co. Mayo.

Many of the towers have an elevated doorway. The purpose was to make entry difficult, but it would not have prevented access. There were no other defensive measures provided to fend off an aggressor who was not deterred by heights.

It is also possible that the elevation of the doorway was designed to preserve the structure of these towers. With shallow foundations, a large opening at ground level could have undermined the entire tower. The towers are usually plain and do not feature religious carvings such as we might see at contemporary churches. Where carvings exist, they are often focused on the doorway and imbue these buildings with religious symbolism.

Aside from a few examples that have modern ladders providing access to the top, most of the round towers are empty shells. Where towers are missing their roof, they might even be mistaken for a chimney.

It is not clear if these towers were rendered on their exteriors. However, it is clear that the interiors were plastered and may also have been painted. This implies that the towers were not simply stair wells to the top bell-floor. Quite likely, each level served a purpose, perhaps as a secure storage place for valuable relics, books and even money (though it is unlikely that they were used as libraries or treasuries). It is also

10 ROUND TOWERS OF IRELAND

possible that some levels were designed to accommodate the private chapel and sleeping quarters of hermits.

It was at the uppermost level, the bell-floor, where the church bell was hung. This part of the tower featured the most windows, usually four, often facing north, east, south and west.

To understand the round towers, we need to consider the period during which they were frequently constructed, i.e., the late 11th century and the first half of the 12th century.

The round towers would have been Ireland's tallest buildings at the time of their construction – taller even than any of the secular buildings commissioned by the most powerful kings. These kings were responsible for the construction of several round towers at church sites that were close to their spiritual hearts. However, in most cases, this royal patronage was likely politically motivated.

An early 12th-century bell discovered at Glendalough, Co. Wicklow, and on display at the National Museum of Ireland, is the only known bell to survive from the period during which the round towers were built.

At the beginning of the 12th century, one powerful king of Munster, Murtaugh O'Brien (Muirchertach Ua Briain), set about transforming the Irish church. In 1101, he convened a synod of church leaders at the Rock of Cashel, Co. Tipperary. The decisions at the Synod of Cashel established clear lines of distinction between the clergy and the laity, lines that had become blurred in previous centuries. This assembly set in motion a reform of the Irish church. Murtaugh presented the Rock of Cashel to the church 'as an offering to St Patrick and to the Lord'. The oldest building on the Rock of Cashel is a round tower, likely commissioned by King Murtaugh.

In 1111 Murtaugh O'Brien convened another synod at Ráth Breasail near Cashel. Plans were drawn up for a diocesan hierarchy of the Irish church, with two metropolitan sees, one in the northern half of Ireland at Armagh, and one in the south at Cashel. This was a momentous event in the history of the Irish church; seventeen of the twenty-four dioceses proposed survive to the present day.

Over the next thirty years, many churches that had been elevated to diocesan status were busy consolidating their new positions. Others that had been overlooked decided to fight for position. The next important synod, reputedly attended by some 3,000 clerics, took place at Kells, Co. Meath and the Cistercian abbey at Mellifont, Co. Louth (only ten years old) in March 1152. The synod was attended by Cardinal John Paparo, who came with important gifts known as pallium (ecclesiastical vestments bestowed by the Pope, symbolising the jurisdiction delegated to primates). Under the agreement with Rome, there would be two new archdioceses, namely Dublin in the east and Tuam in the west, to add to Armagh and Cashel.

Most of the dioceses owe their origins to either the Synod of Ráth Breasail in 1111 or the Synod of Kells in 1152. Church and secular powers were inextricably linked, and the boundaries of the archdioceses reflected those of the provincial kingdoms (Ulster, Leinster, Munster and Connaught), while dioceses reflected the territories of the smaller kingdoms. This period witnessed a turbulent transformation of both secular and church power. Kings of all ranks invested in the ecclesiastical infrastructure to ensure that their favoured church could compete with those of its nearest neighbours. New cathedrals were constructed, ancient relics were enshrined and biographies of the founding saints were compiled – all on a scale never seen before. Round towers were an important element of this new ecclesiastical infrastructure – monuments on an unprecedented scale, symbolising both the spiritual and political ambitions of a given church and bringing its royal patrons and local congregations one step closer to God, and power.

MIDLANDS

ROCK OF CASHEL, CO. TIPPERARY

The great limestone bulk of the Rock of Cashel rises up above the fertile 'Golden Vale', topped with its impressive collection of medieval structures: chapel, cathedral, high cross and round tower.

For centuries the Rock of Cashel had been a symbol of the Eóganacht dynasty of kings who had ruled Munster; the name in Irish *Caiseal na Rí* translates as Cashel of the Kings. Today, no trace of the former royal fortress survives. When Murtaugh O'Brien (Muirchertach Ua Briain), whose family had dominated the kingship of Munster for over a century, donated the Rock to the church in 1101, he effectively decommissioned the royal fortress of his rivals.

The official handover took place during a synod that brought church leaders from all over Ireland to Cashel. Ten years later, Cashel became the seat of a newly created archdiocese that extended across the entire southern half of Ireland, and this newcomer to the ecclesiastical stage rose to become the most important church in Munster.

The oldest building that we can see here today is a round tower, likely commissioned by Murtaugh after 1101, consolidating Cashel's power and position at the 1111 synod of Ráth Breasail. This freestanding tower, 28 m (92 ft) tall, features small putlog holes that were left over from securing the wooden scaffolding used to construct the tower. The round-headed doorway faces south-east, probably in the direction of the west doorway of the church that once stood nearby but was demolished in the 13th century to make way for the present cathedral. In common with many round towers, there are four windows on the top floor for ringing the bell.

The Romanesque chapel of Cormac MacCarthy, king of Munster, consecrated in 1134, on the Rock of Cashel, Co. Tipperary.

The Rock of Cashel round tower viewed from within the cathedral.

ROSCREA, CO. TIPPERARY

Roscrea is believed to have been founded by St Crónán during the middle of the 7th century and is said to have belonged to the Cianachta, ancestors of the O'Carroll and Maher lords of the lands around Roscrea. The Book of Dimma, a gospel book housed in Trinity College Dublin, may have been compiled here at the turn of the 9th century. The round tower was probably constructed in the early 12th century, when Roscrea had ambitions to become the seat of a diocese. Such ambitions attracted the attention of competitors, and the church was reputedly burned on four occasions. The round tower was also struck by lightning in 1135. Despite this prolonged period of unrest, the church was elevated to the status of an episcopal see. At the 1152 Synod of Kells, Roscrea achieved cathedral status. However, within a few decades, Roscrea had been absorbed within the neighbouring diocese of Killaloe.

The round tower we see today is likely to be the same one that was struck by lightning in 1135. The impressive six-storey tower is unusual for having carvings within the second-floor window, depicting a single-masted ship. The tower stands 20 m (65½ ft) tall, but it was originally much taller. According to local tradition, the tower was used by snipers during the 1798 rebellion to attack the British garrison in the nearby castle.

The Black Mills museum behind the tower houses St Crónán's high cross and other artefacts.

Over the centuries, a town has developed around the old monastery at Roscrea, not unlike Killala, Co. Mayo, and today a busy road divides the round tower from the ruins of what was once an impressive Romanesque cathedral, symbolising Roscrea's short-lived episcopal status.

16 ROUND TOWERS OF IRELAND

CLONMACNOISE, CO. OFFALY

Clonmacnoise round tower attached to St Finghin's Church, constructed from the fallen stones of the original early 12th-century tower.

Clonmacnoise is a striking yet peaceful place, particularly when approached by boat. It is here, in 545, that St Ciarán, one of the Twelve Apostles of Ireland, founded what became a major monastery and centre of learning, trade and craftsmanship. The settlement was located close to two key routes, the River Shannon and the east-west thoroughfare of Slíghe Mhór (the Great Road) that brought pilgrims here from across the country. Today, the visitor can see the remains of eight churches, two round towers, and hundreds of early gravestones. The original three high crosses were replaced with replicas in 1991 and are now housed in the interpretative centre.

Turlough O'Conor (Toirrdelbach Ua Conchobhair) was king of Connaught for almost fifty years (1106–1156) and high king of Ireland (c. 1120–1156). He is the first Irish king to have constructed castles in Ireland (eg, at Galway, in 1124), and in 1120 he had a bridge built across the River Shannon at Athlone. The River Shannon was important to Turlough, not just as a boundary between his kingdom of Connaught and that of Meath, but also as the site of

ROUND TOWERS OF IRELAND 17

the monastery of Clonmacnoise. The settlement's siting on the eastern banks of the river, in what might be considered enemy territory, did not dissuade Turlough's spiritual draw to what was one of Ireland's most renowned early churches.

In 1115 Turlough fasted at Clonmacnoise and presented gifts of a silver goblet and a drinking horn decorated with gold. In 1124 he helped pay for the construction of the round tower that still stands there today.

This round tower at Clonmacnoise must once have been one of the tallest towers ever seen in Ireland. However, eleven years after it was built, it was struck by lightning and the top third of the tower collapsed. The finely carved ashlar masonry from this fallen section did not go to waste and, some years later, was recycled to build another tower, attached to the small Romanesque church nearby known as St Finghin's.

Above: The cathedral at Clonmacnoise. When he died in 1156, king of Connaught Turlough O'Conor chose to be buried beside the altar of St Ciarán within the cathedral at Clonmacnoise, near the round tower that he helped to build over thirty years earlier.

Below left: The most famous of the Clonmacnoise high crosses, the Cross of the Scriptures, known as King Flann's Cross. The cross is decorated on four sides, with the west face (depicted) showing the Crucifixion at the top, soldiers guarding Christ's tomb and the arrest and flagellation of Jesus, among other figures.

Below right: An example of one of over 700 early Christian grave slabs discovered at Clonmacnoise.

Constructed c. 1150, the Timahoe round tower is one of the finest surviving examples in the country. It is built with sandstone and limestone blocks and stands nearly 30 m (98 ft) tall, despite leaning precariously to the northwest.

TIMAHOE, CO. LAOIS

The early monastery at Timahoe (*Teach Mo Chua*) is in the ancient territory of Loígse, which gives its name to the modern county of Laois. The site is associated with St Mo Chua (*d.* 657) who it is said came from Connaught and was reported to have been a soldier who became a monk late in life. It is recorded in the *Annals of the Four Masters* that in 1069 Macraith O'More (Ua Mórdha) killed his rival Gilla Muire in the doorway of the church here. This violation of the sanctuary of the church was compounded by the fact that the two men had just sworn an oath on the *Caimmín*, a relic associated with St Mo Chua. Subsequently O'More was killed at nearby Aghaboe with the *Caimmín* in his possession, and his death was seen as a revenge of Mo Chua.

The imposing Timahoe round tower comprises six storeys above a basement level. The bell-floor at the top has four windows with triangular heads that complement the conical cap of the tower. There are few windows at the lower levels, though the floor directly above the doorway has a round-headed window with an architrave and triangular hood, suggesting that this was an important room within the tower and served a function that had nothing to do with bell ringing. The projecting sides of the window frame form columns with carved heads adorning the bases and capitals.

Located some 5 m (16 ft) above the ground is the most elevated and ornamental doorway of all the round towers in Ireland. The doorway comprises two Romanesque doorways. The columns of both doorframes have plain rolled mouldings, but the inner arches are finely carved with lozenge or chevron patterns. The more elaborate carvings are found on the capitals and bases of the columns, featuring male heads with interlocking hair. This was clearly a ceremonial doorway, perhaps a place where important relics such as the *Caimmín* could be displayed at a safe distance from anyone who might wish to run away with it again.

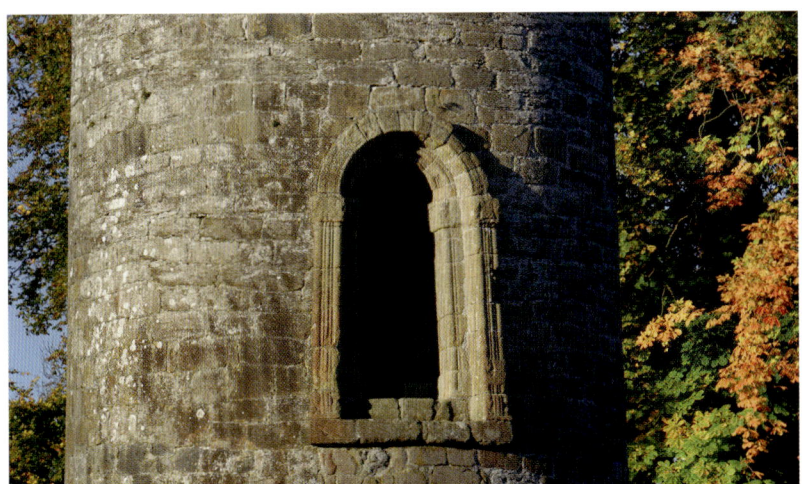

ROUND TOWERS OF IRELAND 21

ST CANICE'S CATHEDRAL, KILKENNY

Kilkenny is rich in surviving late medieval buildings, from churches and friaries to castles and houses. The round tower is the oldest and tallest building in Kilkenny, standing on an elevated site overlooking the River Nore. At the Synod of Ráth Breasail in 1111, the long-established site of St Canice's Church (*Cill Chainnigh*) was selected as the cathedral of the newly formed diocese of Ossory. The round tower may have been commissioned to reflect the site's new status, perhaps with the assistance of the then king of Ossory, Donal Mac Gilla Patrick (Domnall Mac Donnchada Mac Gilla Pátraic).

In 1705, the chapter of the adjoining cathedral paid for the repair of the tower, an early example of a conservation project that has helped ensure its survival to the present day. In 1847, James Graves, a local rector, investigated the ground below the tower, both inside and out. He found that the plinth on which the tower was constructed is only 60 cm (2 ft) deep, which is very little compared to the great height of the tower itself. This is a common feature of round towers throughout the country. The aptly named Graves also discovered that the tower was built directly on top of an older cemetery.

The eight-storey tower in Kilkenny sits alongside St Canice's Cathedral and is a little over 30 m (98 ft) tall. It has the typical elevated doorway, but unusually there are six windows at the top floor. Encircling the top is a parapet, added in the later medieval period. Visitors who climb to the top are rewarded by remarkable city and countryside views, from Mount Leinster in the east to Slievenamon in Tipperary.

GRANGEFERTAGH, CO. KILKENNY

Not far from Johnstown, the round tower at Grangefertagh dominates the surrounding countryside, much as it would have when first constructed. This early ecclesiastical site was dedicated to St Ciarán of Seir Kieran, Co. Offaly, who was one of the most revered saints in the ancient kingdom of Ossory. According to the *Annals of the Four Masters*, the Chief Master was burned in the *cloictheach* (the bell-tower) here in 1156, though the circumstances of how the fire occurred are unclear.

The eight-storey round tower includes the lower portion of its conical stone roof. It stands 31 m (101½ ft) high and has nine windows in all, including four triangular-headed bell-floor windows that face the cardinal points.

In 1880, the tower was saved from destruction and a severe crack that had developed on one side was repaired. The nearby church was re-established in the 13th century as a priory for the Canons Regular of St Augustine. The priory was dissolved in 1540 but continued in use as a Protestant church until 1780, when the roof collapsed. The church fell into ruin and was subsequently used as a handball alley.

In the chapel adjoining the ruins of Grangefertagh Church is a fine tomb featuring the effigies of John Mac Gilla Patrick and his wife Katherine Molloy. The inscription tells us that their son Brian is buried with his parents. The Mac Gilla Patrick family were lords of Ossory and had the chapel built in the mid-16th century. The tomb is an example of the O'Tunney school of sculptors who were prolific throughout Kilkenny and Tipperary during this period.

The imposing Grangefertagh round tower, with its northeast-facing disfigured doorway, just over 3 m (10 ft) from the ground. The stones of the original doorframe were reputedly removed by a local farmer to form a fireplace because he thought they were fireproof, which proved not to be the case.

TULLAHERIN, CO. KILKENNY

The early monastic site of Tullaherin near Thomastown is mentioned in the *Annals of the Four Masters* when the round tower was struck by lightning in 1121, dislodging a stone that fell and killed a student. The church is dedicated to St Ciarán of Seir Kieran, Co. Offaly, who is also associated with Grangefertagh.

The six-storey round tower stands over 22 m (72 ft) tall and measures nearly 5 m (16 ft) in diameter at the base. The doorway faces northeast in the direction of the later medieval church ruins. Unfortunately, the frame of the elevated doorway is entirely missing. There are four small flat-headed windows in the main body of the tower, which is constructed from dressed, finely coursed sandstone blocks. The bell-floor is incomplete and the roof is missing. There are four surviving windows here, but originally there may have been eight. This uppermost portion of the tower is constructed from rubble masonry and is clearly of a later date to the main body of the tower. It may represent a repair of the tower after the lightning strike in 1121, though the bell-floor windows suggest a later medieval date. Beside the tower is an early medieval ogham stone that was found in the late 20th century at nearby Loughboreen, where it had been reused as a gate post. Unfortunately, the inscription is badly defaced and only partly legible.

Tullaherin round tower.

KILREE, CO. KILKENNY

The early church site of Kilree is traditionally associated with St Brigid of Kildare, but during the later medieval period it was held by the Cistercian abbey at Jerpoint, near Thomastown. The round tower is a particularly fine example, standing 29 m (95 ft) tall.

The base of this tower stands on a monolithic rectangular-pad foundation, a feature that is only found with one other round tower in the country, at nearby Aghaviller. The first-floor window has a triangular head, while the remaining three have flat lintels. There are four windows at the bell-floor, facing the cardinal points. The original roof is missing, and the top features battlements that may be late medieval in date.

In the field close by Kilree round tower stands an important example of a high cross, belonging to the regional group the Western Ossory crosses. Other fine examples can be seen at nearby Killamery as well as Ahenny, Co. Tipperary. These are amongst the earliest of the Irish high crosses, thought to date to the beginning of the 9th century.

The round-headed doorway of Kilree round tower is 1.6 m (5 ft) above the ground and faces south towards the door of the nearby church that is slightly older than the tower. Around the doorframe is a raised architrave, a feature of several other towers, such as Drumlane, Co. Cavan and Taghdoe, Co. Kildare.

AGHAVILLER, CO. KILKENNY

The Aghaviller round tower and church lie hidden away in the Kilkenny countryside. The church is traditionally associated with St Brendan (Bréanainn) of Birr, viewed by some as one and the same as the more famous St Brendan of Clonfert, Co. Galway, better known today as St Brendan the Navigator. However, in the late 7th century, these were believed to have been two entirely different people, and our Brendan of Birr at Aghaviller was reputed to have saved Colum Cille from excommunication.

The round tower is the oldest surviving structure here. The tower is well constructed, with a curious mix of sections built with large stones, separated by sections of smaller stones. Some 4 m (13 ft) above the ground is a round-headed doorway, facing the ruins of the nearby medieval church. A later doorway was broken through the bottom of the tower, and this allows visitors to enter the interior without a ladder. The curious ruins of the church can also be explored and make for an atmospheric and memorable visit.

Aghaviller round tower.

ROUND TOWERS OF IRELAND 27

EAST

CLONDALKIN, CO. DUBLIN

Clondalkin was once the site of a monastery founded by St Crónán, one of the seven saintly sons of Lughaidh, a member of a leading family in Leinster. St Crónán is believed to have baptised St Kevin of Glendalough. Indeed, in 790, St Crónán and St Kevin's relics were taken jointly on a circuit around Ireland. There seems little doubt that there was a close connection between Glendalough and Clondalkin during their early years.

The round tower here, with its flat-headed doorway and windows, is thought to be one of the earliest towers constructed in Ireland, possibly in the 11th century. Standing nearly 27 m (88 ft) tall, Clondalkin round tower is the best-preserved example in the Dublin region, complete with its original roof.

Subsequently Clondalkin became attached to the diocese of Dublin, and the significance of this is explored in the other Dublin entries, Lusk and Swords.

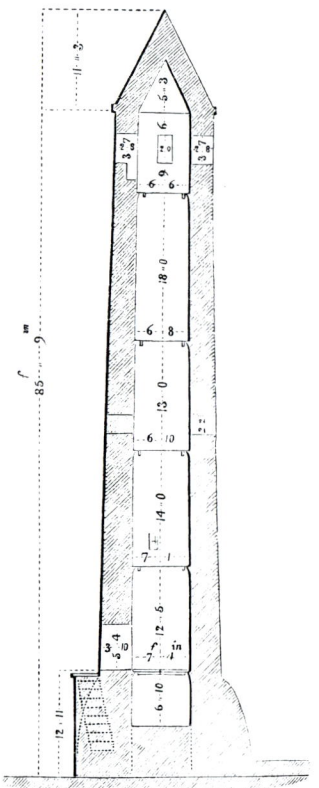

Right: The Clondalkin tower has been refitted with four floors, but we know from an early 19th-century drawing by George Petrie that it originally had five. At some point, a wide buttress was added like a skirt around the base of the tower, and later still, stone steps were added to provide access to the door, concealing the fact that originally it was elevated well above the ground.

Far right: The round tower at Clondalkin is virtually the only surviving remains of what was once an important ecclesiastical site during the early medieval period.

28 ROUND TOWERS OF IRELAND

LUSK, CO. DUBLIN

The church at Lusk, in the area of north county Dublin long known as Fingal, is one of the oldest in the region, apparently founded by Bishop MacCuilinn (*d* 496 or 498). The medieval church at Lusk was demolished in 1847 to make way for the present one, but the 15th-century tower that stood at the west end of the original church still survives today. This five-storey tower is one of the most remarkable late-medieval bell-towers anywhere in the country. It is square in plan, but has round, slender turrets on three of its corners. The fourth corner is a much older round tower, thought to be pre-1100. For centuries this nine-storey tower stood alone as a bell-tower. When the local Anglo-Norman gentry commissioned a new and much larger belfry to serve their parish church, they integrated the older tower into their design, allowing it to rise slightly above the three new corner turrets. However, the round tower was set very slightly apart, retaining the original doorway as the only means of access.

The Lusk round tower was blended with the later 15th-century turrets, which in turn were retained by the 19th-century church building.

ROUND TOWERS OF IRELAND 29

SWORDS, CO. DUBLIN

Swords round tower – one of the round towers to survive in Dublin.

The round tower at Swords is another lofty tower, 26 m (85 ft) tall, but the rubble limestone used in its construction is somewhat inferior compared to the quarried stone used at nearby Lusk. Despite this, the Swords tower has survived nearly a thousand years, though the clumsy top was added in more recent centuries.

The towers at Swords, Lusk and Clondalkin are some of the earliest examples in Ireland, possibly built in the late 11th century, at a time when the bishops of Dublin and their Norse patrons were cementing their areas of influence. Contrary to the belief that the Vikings were raiding ecclesiastical sites, Norse rulers such as the notorious Sitriuc Silkenbeard were consolidating power with links to the church. Nearing his retirement, Sitriuc Silkenbeard undertook a pilgrimage to Rome. On his return he founded Christ Church Cathedral in Dublin, and it became the centre of a new diocese. The round towers of Dublin are thought to reflect the power and influence of the bishops of Dublin and their allied Norse rulers.

GLENDALOUGH, CO. WICKLOW

Glendalough (*Gleann dá Locha*, or Valley of the Two Lakes) was selected by St Kevin (*d. c. 620*) as a hermitage, which in time would grow to become one of the most renowned monasteries throughout Ireland. St Kevin is reputed to have lived the life of a hermit in a cave (St Kevin's Bed) in the cliff above the Upper Lake at Glendalough.

At the end of the 11th century there was an explosion of church building throughout the valley. What makes Glendalough so special is that remnants of churches, other buildings, such as the 12th-century 'Priest's House' (possibly the tomb-shrine of St Kevin), and ancient stones, among them the legendary Deer Stone, are scattered around the two lakes and visitors are immersed in this historic place, with its interpretative centre, ancient traditions and nearby scenic trails.

Pilgrimage was very important to Glendalough, and a road known as St Kevin's Road was constructed to encourage prospective pilgrims to make the journey from west Wicklow and Kildare across the mountains. This pilgrim road continues in use today.

Glendalough may well have been seeking to eclipse its ecclesiastical rival in nearby Dublin. In 1111 Dublin was subsumed into the newly formed diocese of Glendalough. However, Glendalough's status as the seat of a diocese was short-lived. By 1216 Glendalough was fully incorporated into the diocese of Dublin.

For many the most iconic building that survives in the valley is the round tower, which was probably built in the 12th century as part of Glendalough's bid to become a diocese. The tower stands a little over 30 m (98 ft) tall and the round-headed granite doorway faces in the direction of the cathedral. Inside are a series of joist holes, indicating that there were six stages of wooden floors. Windows spiral around the circumference of the tower, one to each floor. The bell-floor has four windows, roughly aligned north, east, south and west. The conical roof was reconstructed in 1876, apparently using the stones from the original one.

Opposite: Glendalough is a stunning ecclesiastical site nestled in a valley of the Wicklow hills.

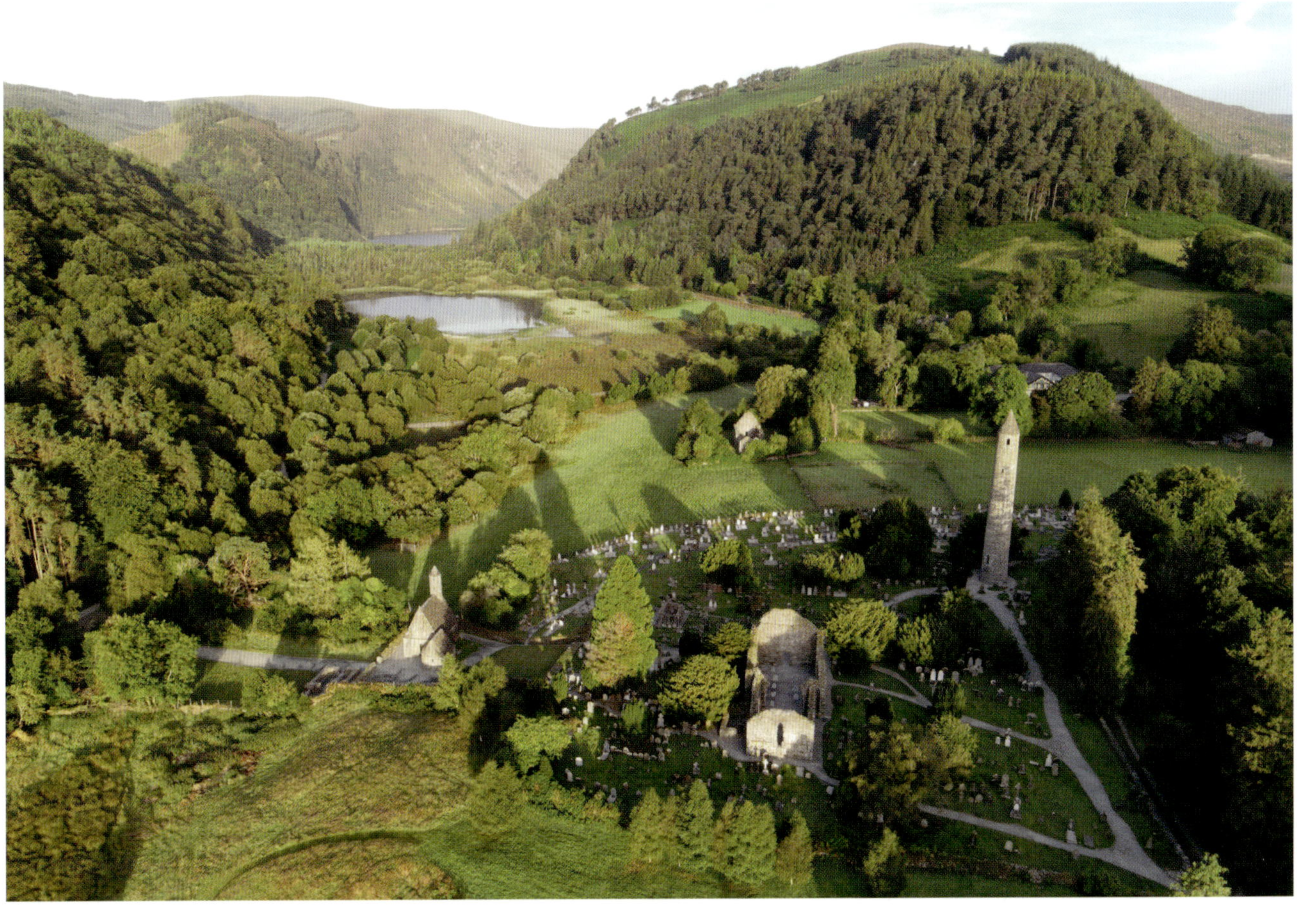
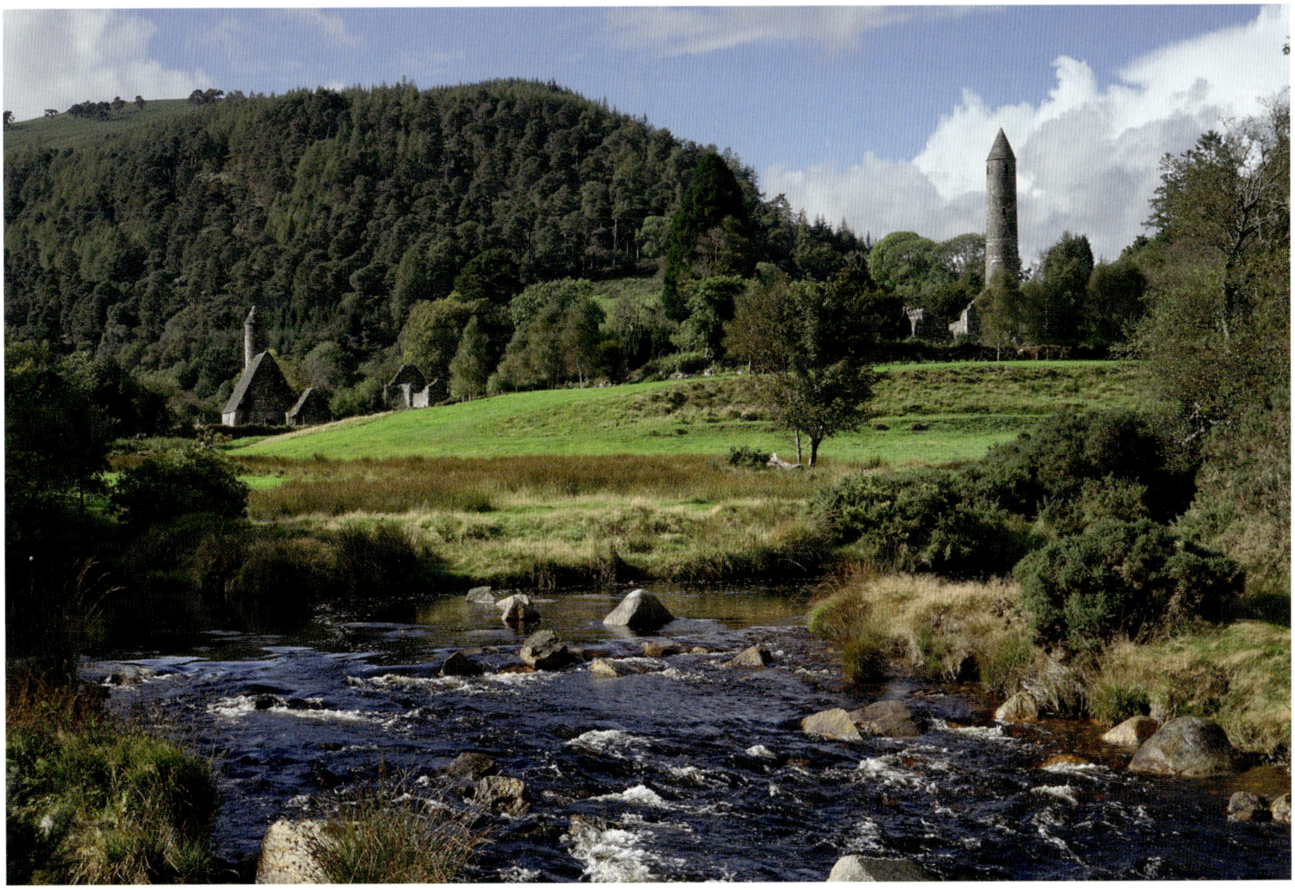

TAGHADOE, CO. KILDARE

Taghdoe in north Kildare takes its name from its founder, St Tua (alias Ultán), who died in 610 while on pilgrimage at Clonmacnoise. Little is known about the early history of this site and the reason a round tower was constructed here at the beginning of the 12th century.

According to tradition, the bottom of the round tower was used to store coal that was used to heat the church when it was in use. During the 12th century the church was held by the bishop of Glendalough, which became the seat of a diocese in 1111. Two other Kildare churches that also feature round towers, namely Castledermot and Old Kilcullen, also formed part of the diocese of Glendalough. It is possible that the bishop sponsored their construction and may suggest that Glendalough had ambitions to become an archdiocese over the entire east of the country.

Above left: The five-storey Taghadoe round tower stands almost 20 m (65½ ft) tall, with carefully laid coursing. Beside the tower is the ruinous shell of a curious Neo-gothic Church of Ireland church, which was built in 1821 and abandoned just forty years later.
Above right: The elevated, round-headed, granite doorway of Taghadoe round tower, 3.5 m (11 ft) from the ground. The right-hand side has been replaced with limestone blocks. The stone above the arch protrudes and may be the weathered remains of a human head.

CASTLEDERMOT, CO. KILDARE

The early church at Castledermot was named after St Dermot (*d*. 825) who belonged to the *Céili Dé* (Clients of God) or Culdee movement, a union of clerics who were devoted to the anchorite way of life, which saw a revival at the turn of the 9th century. The older name of Castledermot was *Díseart Diarmada* (Dermot's Hermitage), implying that the early church here began as a hermitage site. During the 9th and 10th centuries, the annals record the death of several abbots and bishops of Castledermot, including Maelruain (*d*. 884), abbot of Castledermot, who took his name from Maol Ruain of Tallaght near Dublin, the spiritual leader of the *Céili Dé* movement. The most notable abbot during this period was Sneidhius (*d*. 887) who was described as a wise man and tutor of Cormac son of Cullenan (Cormac Mac Cuilennáin), the bishop-king of Munster killed at the battle of nearby Ballaghmoon in 908 and reputedly buried at Castledermot, where his body was said to perform 'signs and miracles'. The implication is that his grave was revered as a shrine.

In 1106 the oak church (*dairthech*) at Castledermot was burned, and it is likely that a new stone church was built to replace it. Beside the present Church of Ireland church, dedicated to St James, is a slender round tower that stands 20 m (65½ ft) high, and probably dates to the turn of the 12th century. The doorway is almost at ground level and is connected by a late medieval vaulted passageway to the adjoining St James's Church. The battlemented top of the tower is unusual and may be part of the rebuilding of the bell-floor in the 18th century to accommodate a new bell. This bell still hangs here and is dated 1735.

The Castledermot round tower, with, beside it, a Romanesque doorway which once belonged to a church constructed here in the mid-12th century.

ROUND TOWERS OF IRELAND 35

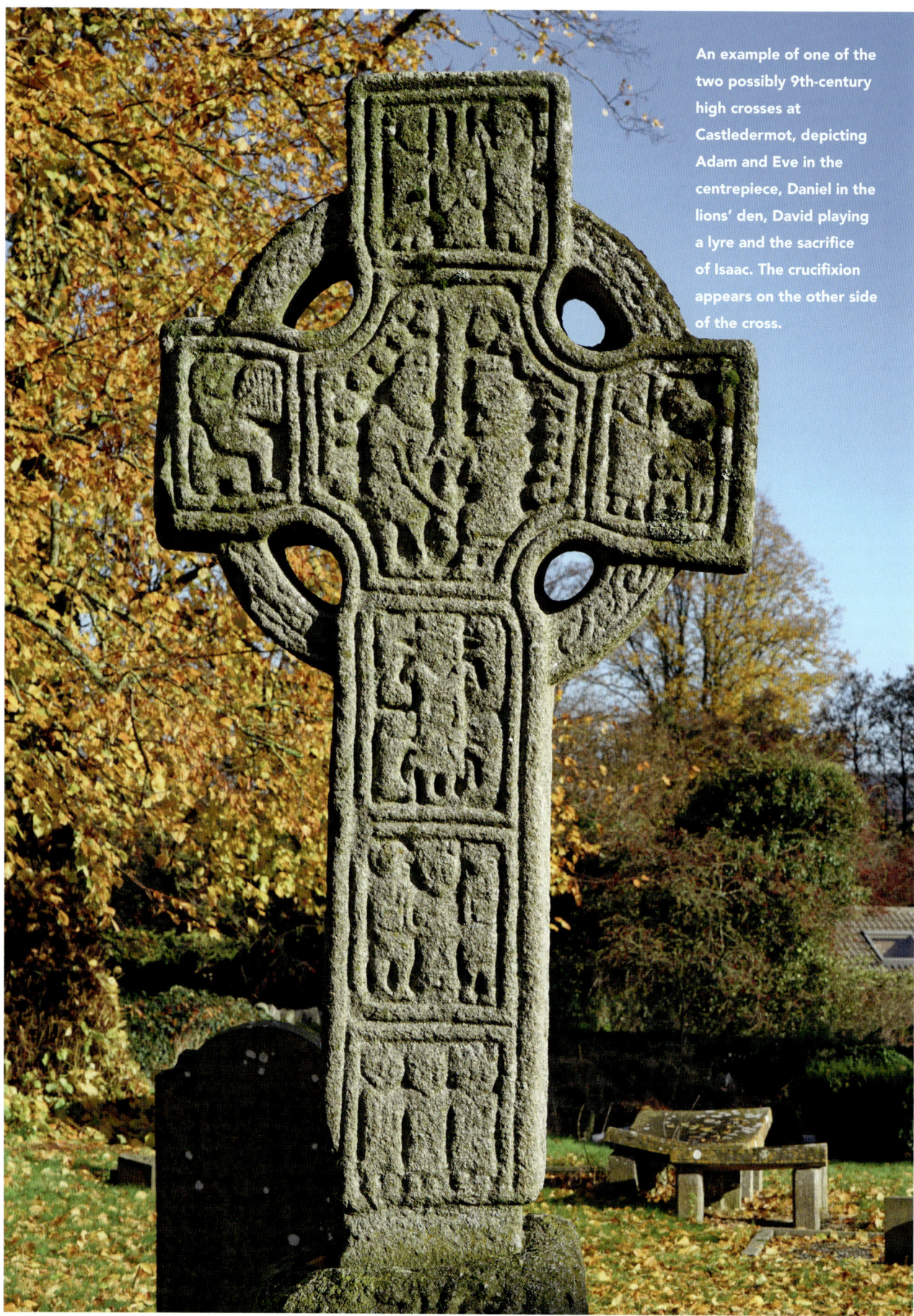

An example of one of the two possibly 9th-century high crosses at Castledermot, depicting Adam and Eve in the centrepiece, Daniel in the lions' den, David playing a lyre and the sacrifice of Isaac. The crucifixion appears on the other side of the cross.

OLD KILCULLEN, CO. KILDARE

Old Kilcullen is an early ecclesiastical site on the summit of a hill with views over the surrounding countryside of south Kildare. This early Christian foundation later became associated with St Patrick but is widely believed to have been founded by St Isernius (*d.* 468) who accompanied Palladius on his mission to Ireland in 431, a year before Patrick arrived in Ireland. Isernius was attracted to this area as, for centuries, the neighbouring hill of Dún Áilline had been an important pagan ceremonial site associated with the inauguration of the kings of Leinster.

Kilcullen was plundered by Amhlaibh Godfridsson and the Norse of Dublin in 938, when 1,000 captives were reputedly taken. In 946 another Norse raid on Kilcullen was led by Amhlaibh Cuarán. Both attacks appear to relate to attempts to extend the Norse influence into the region and undermine the local Leinster kings. While Norse raids such as these have often been used to explain the construction of round towers, the round tower at Kilcullen was built nearly 150 years later. It stands a little over 10 m (32½ ft) high, but a drawing from 1782 shows that it was once much taller. On the north side is an elevated, round-headed doorway that faces the former doorway of a church, which has unfortunately been reduced to its foundations. Nearby is the shaft of a granite high cross, missing its ringed head, but featuring several figurative carvings, including a man holding a crozier and wielding an adze over the head of another man, in a scene that may represent Cain slaying Abel.

The ecclesiastical site of Old Kilcullen. During the 12th century, Kilcullen was part of the estate of the bishop of Glendalough in the heart of the Wicklow Mountains, visible on the horizon to the east.

ROUND TOWERS OF IRELAND 37

ST BRIGID'S CATHEDRAL, KILDARE

Kildare takes its name from the Irish *Cill Dara*, meaning Church of the Oak. Though it is known that many early Irish churches were constructed from oak (including the one at Castledermot in Co. Kildare), here the name refers to an oak tree that stood beside a monastery founded at the turn of the 6th century by St Brigid, the most important saint in Leinster during the early medieval period. Originally founded for nuns, Kildare later became a double monastery, hosting both women and men, answerable to an abbess or abbot respectively. Centuries later, the round tower was built, perhaps to celebrate the elevation of St Brigid's celebrated church to cathedral status at the Synod of Ráth Breasail in 1111.

Visibility is a key theme of virtually every round tower, and the Kildare tower is a prominent landmark throughout the low-lying landscape of the nearby Curragh plains. The lowest section of this fine example of a round tower is constructed using granite ashlar blocks, which

St Brigid's Church of Ireland Cathedral, close to the market square.

stand out from the grey limestone used to construct the major portion of the tower. Unfortunately, the sandstone doorway is very badly defaced. The battlemented roof level, as at Castledermot, was added in the 18th century. Interestingly, the top of the tower was one of thirty-two trigonometrical stations that formed the basis for the triangulation of Ireland as part of the Ordnance Survey's ambitious mapping of the country between 1824 and 1846.

Left: The round tower at Kildare is the second tallest of the surviving towers and is open to the public during the summer. Below: Originally the Kildare round tower was one of the finest of any tower in the country, and we get a sense of the richness of the Romanesque carvings from those that have survived under the protection of the inner arch.

ROUND TOWERS OF IRELAND 39

OUGHTERARD, CO. KILDARE

Ougherard takes its name from the Irish *Uachtar Árd*, meaning the High Upper Place, and this is one of the highest hills in east Kildare. Such an elevated location is a feature of several early church sites in the region. That this was one of the earlier Christian foundations is suggested by its association with St Brigid, whose main site is at nearby Kildare. The oldest feature that we see today is the remains of a round tower that stands less than 10 m (32½ ft) tall and must be a shadow of its former self. The round-headed doorway is a little over 2.5 m (8 ft) from the ground, and only one window survives above. The site is perhaps best known as the burial place of Ireland's infamous brewer, Arthur Guinness (*d.* 1803).

Oughterard round tower.

DROMISKIN, CO. LOUTH

The church at Dromiskin was associated with St Rónán and would later become the centre of a manor of the archbishop of Armagh. The scale of the round tower here is more in keeping with the Spanish windmills at Campo de Criptana that Don Quixote might have charged in the mistaken belief they were ferocious giants. Standing just 15 m (49 ft) high today, it is likely that this was originally a much taller tower. The conical-shaped stone roof is true to the original form, but internally there are traces of a wicker frame used in its construction, a technique used by later medieval masons. The Romanesque doorway, carved from red sandstone, has two plain receding arches and dates from the mid-12th century. The outer arch originally sprang from circular columns that are unfortunately now missing. Such columns can be found at doorways of several Romanesque churches, but this is the only example from a round tower.

Dromiskin round tower.

MONASTERBOICE, CO. LOUTH

Monasterboice in County Louth was dedicated to St Buithe who died around 520 and was closely associated with one of Ireland's greatest saints, Colum Cille. One story about Buithe recounts that he brought back to life a man who had been beheaded by the high king of Ireland. The fortunate man spent his remaining days tending to the monastic garden at Monasterboice. Ironically, it was Buithe's own head that would be the monastery's greatest relic, until it was stolen from the church in 1520, a thousand years after his death. During the early medieval period Monasterboice was a centre of learning and literature, as reflected in the obituary of one of its clerics, Flann Mainistreach, who died in 1056. He was described in the annals as lector of Monasterboice and master of 'wisdom, literature, history, poetry and science'. In 1097, the bell-tower of Monasterboice was burnt, resulting in the destruction of the monastery's

Near the foot of the round tower at Monasterboice is one of two monumental stone crosses. Appropriately known as the Tall Cross, it stands 7 m (23 ft) high and is the tallest cross in Ireland.

books and treasures. This account has always been taken to refer to the round tower that we see here today. However, it is more likely that the present tower dates to the early 12th century and replaced whatever bell-tower was damaged in 1097.

The present six-storey tower stands over 28 m (91½ ft) high but given that much of the bell-floor and roof is missing, this originally was one of the tallest towers ever constructed. The elevated doorframe is decorated with an architrave and faces the ruins of the adjoining church. So too does a small triangular-headed window on the floor above.

The second cross at Monasterboice stands some 5 m (16½ ft) tall and is arguably the finest example of a high cross anywhere in Ireland. An inscription in Irish at the base of the shaft commemorates Muiredach, abbot of Monasterboice (d. 924). Both Monasterboice crosses were apparently carved by the same sculptor(s) responsible for the 'tower cross' at Kells.

DONAGHMORE, CO. MEATH

There are many placenames throughout Ireland that feature the word *domhnach*, an early Irish word for church that derives from the Latin *dominicum*. In an Irish context, this term invariably denotes a church that was established during the initial conversion era, and here at Donaghmore, near Navan, the church was traditionally associated with St Patrick, who is closely linked to many churches along the nearby River Boyne. Standing nearly 27 m (88½ ft) tall, this is a well-built tower, constructed using limestone blocks.

Lighting one of the floors above the doorway is a small, triangular-headed window. The frame of this window is built with sandstone, which was also used to construct the Romanesque doorway. At first glance this Romanesque feature might indicate a mid-12th-century date for the tower,

The intriguing tower of Donaghmore occupies a fine site overlooking the infamous River Boyne, with a well-tended graveyard and the remains of a medieval church.

44 ROUND TOWERS OF IRELAND

Directly above the doorway of Donaghmore round tower is a carving of the crucifixion, which is unique for an Irish round tower, although there is one at one of Scotland's two round towers, at Brechin in Angus.

but close examination of the masonry around the doorway suggests that the doorway is not an original feature but instead a later insertion. Another unusual feature of the tower is the lack of any windows at the top where we might expect to find them lighting the bell-floor.

However, we know that the top of the tower, including the roof, was repaired in 1841 by the local landowner and it seems that the windows were removed or infilled at this time. Elsewhere we have seen that many round towers continued to be used as bell-towers throughout the later medieval period and even up to the present day. Therefore, it is striking that during the late medieval period the church here was furnished with a pair of bells that hung in a double bellcote, implying that the round tower was not used for bell ringing during this period.

ROUND TOWERS OF IRELAND 45

KELLS, CO. MEATH

St Columcille (sometimes known by the Latin version of his name, Columba) is one of Ireland's most famous early saints. Born in Donegal, he later went into self-imposed exile in Scotland, founding a monastery on the island of Iona, which would become important in the spread of Christianity throughout northern Britain. Years after his death in 597, in the face of Viking raids that ravished Iona at the turn of the 9th century, some of the community moved to Kells in Co. Meath and established a monastery that they dedicated to Columcille. They brought many relics and other treasures from Iona, including the world-famous illuminated gospel known as the Book of Kells, now on display at Trinity College Dublin.

The monastery is also known for an important collection of high crosses, three in the churchyard of today's Church of Ireland church close by the impressive 26-metre (85-foot) tall round tower, with another, the Market Cross, in the town centre. They were most likely commissioned to celebrate Kells' recognition as the chief monastery of a confederation of churches across Ireland with links to Columcille. This type of confederation was the antithesis of the geographically defined dioceses that were introduced during the 12th-century reforms of the

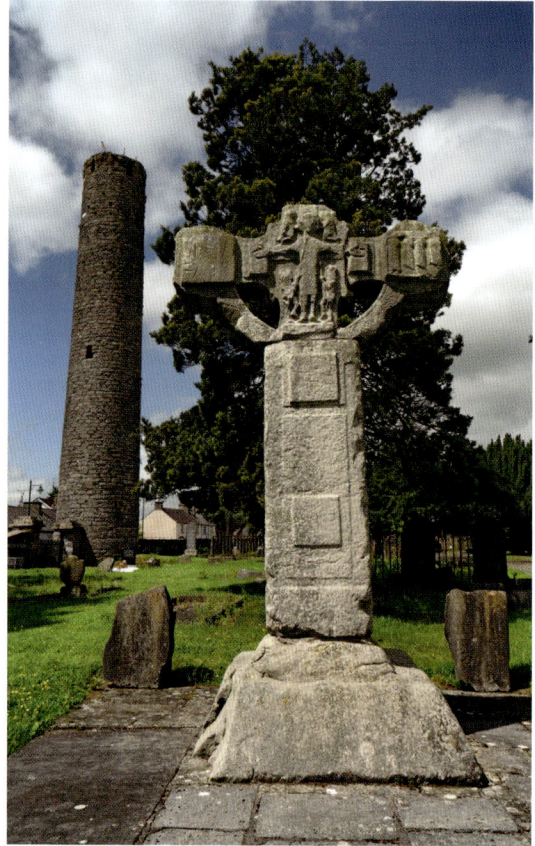

**Opposite bottom left: The Chi Ro page from the Book of Kells, detailing the beginning of the Gospel according to St Matthew.
Opposite bottom right: The well-preserved Kells round tower, which is unusual in that the bell-floor has five windows instead of the more usual four. Nearby is the East or Unfinished Cross, which represents a rare example of the early stages in the process of sculpting a high cross.
Right: The cross which stands in the shadow of the tower is known as the 'tower cross'. The name is somewhat unwarranted, as this high cross and the others stood here for nearly two centuries before the tower was constructed.**

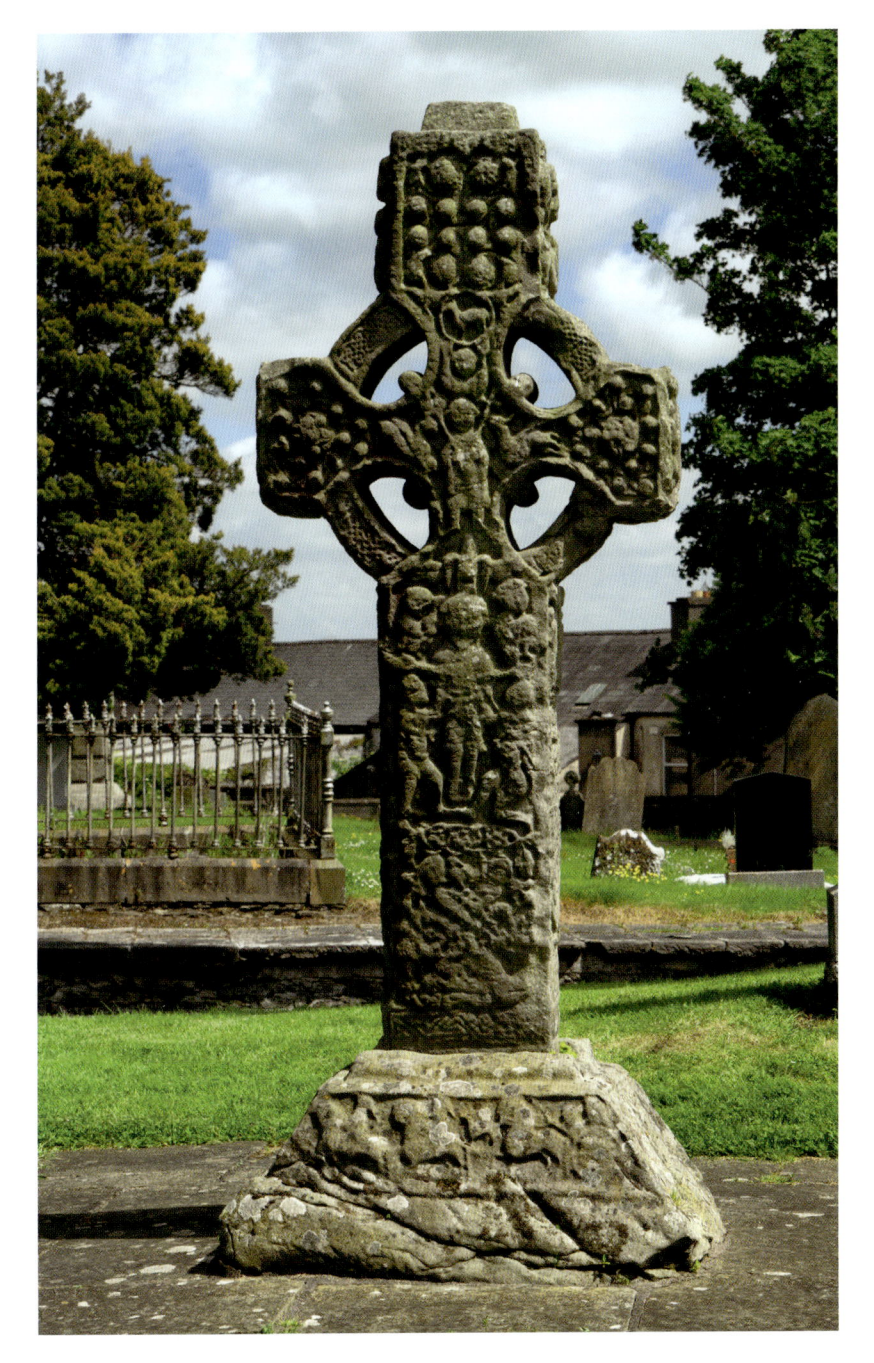

Irish church. Yet, it was here that the infamous synod of 1152 convened to agree the diocesan structure we have today.

In 1076 a remarkable event occurred at Kells, in which Murchadh Máel Sechnaill, king of Tara, was murdered in the bell-tower. This has often been cited as evidence that round towers were used as places of refuge. However, it is not clear that Máel Sechnaill was seeking refuge in tower; it is possible that his stay was intended as penance. His murder may not even have taken place within the tower that we see today, which appears to have been constructed some twenty-five years later.

ROUND TOWERS OF IRELAND 47

SOUTH

ARDMORE, CO. WATERFORD

Above and opposite: Soaring over the ruined cathedral and the surrounding graveyard, the tower at Ardmore can be seen throughout the surrounding countryside and is also very visible by sea.

Later stories state that Ardmore's founder, St Declan (St Déaglán), visited Rome where he received episcopal orders from the Pope himself, and on his return journey he met St Patrick, who hadn't yet undertaken his mission to Ireland. When Declan returned home one of his first actions was to visit Cashel, which became the seat of an archdiocese in 1111. These stories are preserved in a biography known as a Life, written in Latin during the late 12th century, which was clearly designed to elevate the importance of Declan, and by default, his church here.

Though Ardmore was never officially recognised as a bishopric, we can see physical expressions of that ambition with the remains of a Romanesque cathedral and arguably the finest round tower ever built in Ireland.

Standing nearly 30 m (98 ft) tall, it is also quite possibly the last such tower built, constructed at the very end of the 12th century. More than most, the Ardmore tower can be seen clearly narrowing as it rises, and this was achieved by building sections that step in at three intervals, each interval clearly marked by a string coursing (though these are decorative rather than structural). It is constructed with blocks of sandstone, a technique known as ashlar, which was also used to construct the tower on the Rock of Cashel. According to folklore these were somewhat miraculously brought from a quarry some 8 km (5 m) away without the use of a horse or a wheel, and the tower was completed without the sound of a hammer. In fact, the masonry shows clear signs of hammer dressing, and it is highly unlikely that the masons completed their work in silence. The doorframe has roll moulding of a type that was fashionable towards the end of the 12th century. Internally there are several decorative corbels, but these have not been examined in detail and their function remains unclear.

CLOYNE, CO. CORK

Standing over 800 years, the round tower is the oldest and still the tallest building in the small town of Cloyne in east Cork. The church here was founded around the turn of the 6th century by Colmán son of Léinín, who reputedly was a layman for much of his life (possibly a professional poet) before taking holy orders. Little is known of the early history of this site, but it was elevated to cathedral status at the synod of Kells in 1152, though the tower predates this by some fifty years.

Cloyne tower is a truly magnificent tower, standing nearly 30 m (98 ft) in height, with seven storeys above the basement, the space below the elevated doorway. The battlemented parapet seems to have been added to the top of the tower shortly after it was damaged by a lightning strike in January 1749. The bishop of Cloyne at the time was George Berkeley (*d*. 1753), a renowned philosopher of the age, who described the accompanying thunderclap as the loudest he had ever heard, and he wrote that the lightning strike caused the former bell to crash down through the wooden floors below.

Now separated by one of town's principal streets, the Cloyne round tower looks across to the medieval cathedral that continues in use today. The tower is one of a small number of towers that still serves its original purpose, and a bell manufactured by Sheridan's Foundry of Dublin in 1857 continues to hang at the bell-floor.

KINNEIGH, CO. CORK

The round tower at Kinneigh is different from every other example in the country in that its lower section, some 6 m (19½ ft), is not round but hexagonal. Above this very solid base, the tower resumes its conventional cylindrical shape where we can see four small windows, one to each floor above the doorway. The top of the tower is missing, although until quite recently it was still used as a belfry for the adjoining St Bartholomew's Church, built in 1856 in a neo-Romanesque style.

Built using local slate, the Kinneigh round tower stands a little over 20 m (65½ ft) tall, but the builders were able to exaggerate the height by constructing it on an outcrop of rock.

RATTOO, CO. KERRY

For a county rich in early medieval ecclesiastical remains, it is surprising that there are only two round towers known in Kerry, one at Aghadoe near Killarney, the other at Rattoo near Listowel, marking the site of a church founded centuries earlier by St Lughach. During the 19th century, a stone wall was built to enclose the graveyard around the ruined medieval church. The round tower now stands alone outside the graveyard. This is one of the more complete and best-preserved towers in the country, standing nearly 27 m (88½ ft) tall, including the conical roof, though this has been substantially repaired in modern times. Constructed with a warm yellow sandstone, there are six floor levels indicated by rings of projecting corbels. The round-headed doorway faces southeast and has an architrave around the frame that is decorated with curved spirals. The bell-floor at the top has four windows, roughly facing the cardinal points.

A feature unique to this round tower is a shee-la-na-gig, carved on the interior of the north window on the bell-floor. Such explicit carvings are often falsely claimed to represent fertility images, but in fact they symbolised something quite different. These were intended to warn against the sins of the flesh, and more commonly were placed in plain sight for everyone to see. In this case, the only person who would see this was the man charged with ringing the bell.

Rattoo round tower, striking in its construction of yellow sandstone.

DYSERT AENGHUSA, CO. LIMERICK

Dysert Aenghusa near Croom was a monastery belonging to the *Céili Dé* or 'Clients of God', a union of clerics devoted to the anchorite way of life. The church was dedicated to Bishop Aonghas, who was also associated with the spiritual home of the *Céili Dé* at Tallaght, Co. Dublin. He is credited with authorship of a martyrology known as *Féilire Aonghasa*, which recorded the feast days and details of the lives of Ireland's early saints. The name Dysert derives from the Irish word *díseart*, a term borrowed from Latin to describe a deserted place that offered solitude for a monk or cleric seeking to dedicate a period of their life to spiritual contemplation and prayer.

The round tower stands a little over 20 m (65½ ft) tall, but the bell-floor and roof are missing. It was constructed with grey limestone, while red sandstone was used to carve the doorframe and windows. Today, a modern staircase provides visitors with access to the elevated doorway and the first floor. Wooden floors have also been inserted within the tower and give a clear impression of how these would once have appeared.

Recent archaeological investigations at the

Dysert Aenghusa round tower.

The doorway of Dysert Aenghusa round tower is decorated with simple domed discs or bosses around the arch, a feature of several 12th-century Romanesque Irish churches.

base of the tower revealed that it was built on an area of the site that had been used for burials, since at least the 11th century. This has also been revealed at other sites and was used by early commentators to argue that round towers were designed as sepulchral monuments. However, these burials were already centuries old by the time round towers were first built; many sites continue as burial grounds today.

WEST

INIS CEALTRA, CO. CLARE

St Caimín's Church and round tower on Inis Cealtra, Lough Derg, Co. Clare. Today the site feels isolated, but in its heyday it would have been at the centre of a major highway, the Shannon river.

Near the south-western shores of Lough Derg, Inis Cealtra is one of the most striking island monasteries in Ireland. This extraordinary place retains an air of tranquillity. Referred to by the locals as Holy Island, it was historically known as Inis Cealtra and dedicated to St Caimín (d. 651) though it may have been originally founded a century earlier. This island monastery attracted a lot of unwanted attention from the Vikings of Limerick in 837 and 922, who easily reached the lake by sailing up the River Shannon. During the 11th and 12th centuries, the island was one of several important spiritual homes of the O'Brien (Uí Briain) kings of Munster who dominated the Irish political stage at that time. The king Murtagh O'Brien (Muirchertach Ua Briain) had a palace at nearby Killaloe, and he may have commissioned the round tower here at Inis Cealtra.

The heart of the site centres around a church

known as St Caimín's Church. Originally a simple church, built in the 11th century, it was modified during the 12th century with Romanesque sculptures, including a doorway, chancel arch and altar. Between the original construction of this church and its Romanesque refurbishment, the round tower was constructed nearby. Standing a little over 22 m (72 ft) high, it is believed that it may once have been taller. The tower is still a striking landmark for anyone boating on the lake and may have been partly designed as a beacon to pilgrims approaching this ancient monastery.

The long shadow of the round tower crossing the Romanesque doorway of St Caimín's Church on Inis Cealtra.

The island is also home to a small Romanesque church dedicated to St Brigid, a Romanesque shrine chapel known as *Teampall na bhFear nGonta* (Church of the Wounded Men) and a late medieval parish church dedicated to St Mary.

The Saint's Graveyard to the east of the church is a fine example of an early medieval cemetery reserved for the burial of ecclesiastics. The site also has some of the most important remains of early medieval cross-inscribed grave slabs in the country.

SCATTERY ISLAND, CO. CLARE

In the Shannon estuary near Kilrush is Scattery Island, or Inis Cathaigh. A church was founded here by St Senan (Seanán), who legend has it expelled a monster, the serpent Cathagh, from the island. According to a later tradition, when St Ciarán threw his vestment into the River Shannon at Clonmacnoise, it washed up unscathed on the shores of Scattery. During the 12th century, the church here became the seat of a diocese, but it was later subsumed with the diocese of Killaloe. The round tower reflects this ambition, overlooking the ruins of the cathedral dedicated to St Mary and St Senan. There is also a small church nearby dedicated to St Senan, and nearer to the harbour is Templenamarve – 'the Church of the Dead'.

The 26-metre (85-feet)-tall tower on Scattery Island is unusual with its door at ground level, making it one of the most accessible in the country. The steep conical roof is truncated at the top. The bell-floor has the usual four windows facing the cardinal points, and five small windows light different levels below.

It is possible in the summer months to get a boat out to Scattery Island, inhabited until the 1970s and steeped in legend and stories. Visitors can explore several churches, some well preserved, some in ruins, the lighthouse, the Napoleonic artillery battery and the restored farmhouses.

Scattery Island and round tower.

DRUMCLIFFE, CO. CLARE

There is no remaining evidence of a doorway at the Drumcliffe round tower, and it is possible that a weakness in the doorframe caused this side of the tower to slump as it fell, resulting in the unusual appearance that we see today.

Today, Drumcliffe is a vast cemetery, which has served the inhabitants of the nearby town of Ennis for centuries. Overlooking the cemetery is the oldest part of the site, dedicated to a local saint, St Conall. Beside the remains of a late medieval church is a round tower, standing little more than 11 m (36 ft) tall, which evidently suffered a catastrophic collapse. The character of the masonry at the bottom of the tower, which incorporates some very large stones, is noticeably different from the smaller stones used higher up, suggesting that the bottom is somewhat older.

DYSERT O'DEA, CO. CLARE

Near the picturesque village of Corrofin is the equally charming church of Dysert O'Dea, formerly known as Díseart Tola, named after a little-known saint who died in 738. As we can see at other round tower sites, the name Dysert derives from the Irish word *díseart*, a term used to describe a deserted place. This may have been true when the church was originally founded here in the 8th century, but by the time the round tower was built, this was no longer an isolated site. In fact, there was a significant amount of investment in the church here during the 12th century, including the carving of a stunning high cross and the construction of a remarkable Romanesque church (though the latter was subsequently demolished and reassembled as a veritable life-size jigsaw puzzle with all the pieces in the wrong places).

A rare example of a 12th-century crozier from this site is in the National Museum of Ireland. The round tower has largely collapsed but what survives suggests that it was built during the mid-12th century. The upper section steps in suddenly, which is not a feature of any other round tower, and it has been suggested that this portion was constructed during the later medieval period. Much of the original tower may have either collapsed or been taken down, to be rebuilt, only to fall once again.

Dysert O'Dea Church and round tower.

The jumbled human and animal heads on the south doorway of Dysert O'Dea Church.

Dysert O'Dea high cross.

KILMACDUAGH, CO. GALWAY

The round tower at Kilmacduagh is perhaps best known as Ireland's answer to the famous leaning tower of Pisa in Italy. Despite its precarious tilt, the tower stands over 34 m (111½ ft) high, making it one of the tallest ever constructed. Around 1878, the tower was restored by the Office of Public Works and investigations at the time revealed that the foundations were not only very shallow, but the ground beneath was also not very solid. The reason simply being that the tower was built on an ancient cemetery. Therefore, like so many towers elsewhere, when it was built at the beginning of the 12th century, the site had already been long used as a burial ground. In fact, the builders may have been fully aware of the poor ground conditions. At the base is a wide plinth to spread the weight of the tower, while the doorway is almost 8 m (26 ft) above the ground, higher than any other round tower. The builders clearly knew that a doorway nearer the ground would weaken the entire structure.

The church here was originally founded around the turn of the 7th century by St Colman Mac Duach, on land granted by a local king. The church quickly grew in importance but was overlooked as an episcopal see at the Synod of Ráth Breasail in 1111. It is possible that the tower was commissioned in defiance of this. If so, the tactic was successful, and at the Synod of Kells in 1152, Kilmacduagh became the seat of a bishopric. Today, the ruins of the cathedral stand in the shadow of the tower, while nearby are the remains of several other churches, including a priory of canons regular of St Augustine.

Kilmacduagh, Ireland's leaning tower of Pisa. The Kilmacduagh tower is seven storeys high, each floor lit by a single triangular window, except for the upper-most level, which has six.

KILBENNAN, CO. GALWAY

This early church site is located close to Tuam, the seat of an archdiocese established at the 1152 synod of Kells. It is dedicated to St Benan (Beinéan), also known as Benignus, who died in 467, and was St Patrick's successor at Armagh. Given its proximity to Tuam, it is tempting to suggest that this tower was commissioned by Turlough O'Conor (Toirrdelbach Ua Conchobhair), who was the patron of the round tower constructed at Clonmacnoise. Though much of the 16 m (52 ft) high tower is missing, it still overshadows the ruins of the adjoining medieval church. A single stone carved with Romanesque decoration is all that remains of what may have been an elaborate church constructed several decades after the tower was completed.

Constructed almost exclusively using local limestone, special attention was given to the round-headed, carved sandstone doorway of the round tower at Kilbennan.

ROSCAM, CO. GALWAY

Situated on the northern shores of Galway Bay, looking south across to the Burren in Clare, Roscam is an interesting and little studied early medieval church site. The round tower stands a little isolated from other early ecclesiastical remains and there can be little doubt that this was originally a large and complex site. It was reputedly founded by St Odran, a brother of St Ciarán of Clonmacnoise. The tower stands 11 m (36 ft) tall and was well constructed with local limestone blocks. Internal corbels and joist holes reflect four floor levels within. An interesting feature preserved here is the many small holes visible on the exterior. Known as putlog holes, these were used by the original builders to secure their timber scaffolding that wrapped around the outside of the tower. Over time, the timber simply rotted away, leaving the voids we see here at Roscam today. Such timber scaffolding was likely the standard technique used by the builders of round towers, but frequently these tell-tale holes were infilled by subsequent generations.

The doorway of the Roscam round tower, with its flat lintel, faces southeast across a green field, where a church perhaps once stood.

ROUND TOWERS OF IRELAND

KILLALA, CO. MAYO

Towards the end of the 7th century, Bishop Tírachán of Killala wrote one of the earliest biographies of St Patrick, solidifying the links between north Mayo and Ireland's premier saint. This effectively brought much of Connaught under the influence of Armagh, which continues to use its own Patrician connections to claim primacy over all Ireland.

In more recent centuries, a small town has developed around the old cathedral at Killala, utterly changing the character of what was once a large ecclesiastical complex that likely featured several other churches and ecclesiastical buildings. The round tower is the most obvious monument from this period, and its present detached position in relation to the cathedral demonstrates just how much of the original site is missing.

The elevated location of the Killala tower led to a near devastating lightning strike during the 19th century. An obvious bulge on the side of the tower is said to be the result of this incident and it is likely that many of the fragmentary Irish round towers were damaged by such lightning storms. Today the risk of such damage has been averted at Killala by the placement of a lightning conductor on the roof, a feature that has been installed at virtually all complete towers around the country.

A unique 15th-century depiction of a round tower, carved onto the side of the piscina within the church at Rosserk Franciscan friary, is presumed to refer to the nearby tower at Killala.

Built on the highest point in the town, the Killala round tower dominates the skyline of the town and Killala Bay.

AGHAGOWER, CO. MAYO

Aghagower derives its name from the Irish *Achaidh Fobhair*, the 'Field of the Spring', and became the principal church in the ancient territory of Umhall in west Mayo. It is first mentioned at the end of the 7th century in the Life of St Patrick by Tírechán, who is reputed to have visited here prior to his stay at Croagh Patrick, and before leaving he ordained Senach and consecrated a church here, establishing a link between Aghagower and Mayo's holy mountain from this early stage.

Looming over the ruins of the late medieval church is a round tower that stands almost 16 m (53 ft) tall. The original round-headed door is at first-floor level and faces east, in the direction of the church (there is a modern entrance at ground level on the north-west side and visitors can easily get a view of the tower's interior). The rounded arch of the doorway indicates an early 12th-century date, and the stones forming the frame show evidence of fire damage, suggesting that the tower may have been attacked in antiquity. Inside the tower are five rings of projecting corbels, which would have supported the wooden floors. According to tradition, the top of the tower was destroyed by lightning at the beginning of the 19th century.

Left: Aghagower round tower.
Right: The capstone of Aghagower round tower, to be found in the grounds of the adjoining St Patrick's Catholic church, is a rare survival and few are known elsewhere in the country. The stone is conical, which would have complemented the shape of the roof, and there is a small socket at the top, in which a cross of stone or perhaps wood was likely inserted.

MEELICK, CO. MAYO

The church site near Swinford is traditionally associated with St Brocaidh, reputedly a nephew of St Patrick. This association implies that Meelick originally formed part of the network of Patrician foundations that spread throughout the region during the 6th and 7th centuries, and it is interesting that several of these sites, namely Killala, Aghagower and Turlough, feature round towers. Therefore, rather than viewing these towers in isolation, it is worth considering them collectively. Indeed, it is tempting to see them as a monumental expression by the bishop of Killala to establish an expansive diocese in the region at the beginning of the 12th century.

If so, the tactic failed and Meelick, Turlough and Aghagower were not included within the boundaries of the diocese of Killala agreed at the Synod of Ráth Breasail in 1111.

The Meelick tower stands a modest 21.5 m (70 ft) high, but its elevated position on top of a drumlin hill gives an impression that it is much taller. The round-headed doorway of the tower is placed at first-floor level and faces the location of the former church, which no longer survives. In common with all other round towers, the internal floors were originally wooden ones supported on offsets or corbels.

Left: The first floor at Meelick round tower features a rare example of a stone-corbelled ceiling, with a small hole for a ladder that allowed access to the wooden floors above.
Right: At the base of Meelick round tower is a plinth on which the tower is constructed. This is a common feature of many round towers, but the shallow groove incised on the plinth, forming a continuous circle around the circumference, is unusual. Presumably this provided the builders with a guide to position the initial course of masonry for the tower.

ROUND TOWERS OF IRELAND 67

Meelick round tower. An interesting early medieval cross-slab found in the adjoining graveyard at Meelick can be seen attached to the external wall face of the round tower.

TURLOUGH, CO. MAYO

Complete with its conical roof and just 22 m (72 ft) tall, Turlough round tower is one of the shortest towers in the country, but its stocky appearance still dominates the adjoining 17th-century church ruin.

The old graveyard at Turlough, not far from the National Museum of Country Life, is thought to be on the site of a monastery founded by St Patrick, which may explain why the church here was still contested by Armagh until the beginning of the 13th century. The cemetery remains in use. However, the only structure from this early period of the site's history still standing is the round tower. The round-headed doorway, now blocked up, is elevated well above the ground and the uppermost floor, where the bell was rung, has four triangular-headed windows. From the top of the tower, the bell ringer had a view to Croagh Patrick in the distance.

ROUND TOWERS OF IRELAND 69

DRUMCLIFF, CO. SLIGO

Drumcliff, 'under bare Ben Bulben's head', is the last resting-place of Ireland's great poet, W.B. Yeats, beside St Columba's Church of Ireland church, built in 1809. The round tower and the crosses here are the only visible remains of an important monastery, which St Columcille is said to have founded here around 574. According to the *Annals of the Four Masters* the round tower was struck by lightning in 1396. Today the tower reaches just 9 m (29½ ft) tall, probably only a third of its original height, but whether the missing portion can be attributed to the historic lightning strike is unclear, and one legend records that masonry from the tower was used to construct a nearby bridge in the early 19th century. Drumcliff round tower stands somewhat forlorn and divorced from its original ecclesiastical setting, a busy road now cutting through the site.

Beside Drumcliff graveyard is an interesting high cross, probably sculpted a century or so before the round tower was constructed. The carvings include various recognisable Biblical scenes, including David and Goliath, Adam and Eve, Daniel in the Lions' Den and a camel.

70 ROUND TOWERS OF IRELAND

Drumcliff round tower, with Sligo's Ben Bulben rising up in the distance.

NORTH

ANTRIM, CO. ANTRIM

Near the shores of Lough Neagh in the grounds of the appropriately named Steeple Park is one of the finest round towers in Ulster. The parkland setting that has grown up around the tower can be confusing for visitors today and masks the fact that it was part of an early ecclesiastical site associated with Comhghall (*d.* 601/602), founder of Bangor, Co. Down, around the middle of the 6th century. Though perhaps not a well-known figure today, throughout the early medieval period Comhghall was widely regarded as one of the 'holy founders' of the early Irish church.

While the remainder of the church site at Antrim has disappeared, the round tower is one of the most intact anywhere in Ireland. It stands 28 m (92 ft) tall, including its conical roof, which was rebuilt after it was damaged by lightning in 1819. The masonry is crudely constructed, using local basalt, for which Ulster is famous. The door faces northeast, providing a clue as to the likely location of the former church. At the top, the bell-floor is lit by the usual four windows facing the cardinal points.

An unusual carving of a ringed cross can be seen above the granite doorframe of Antrim round tower. Another feature of the doorway is the severe cracking of the sill and the lintel, reflecting the stress caused by the massive weight of the body of the tower.

ARMOY, CO. ANTRIM

Armoy round tower stands just 11 m (36 ft) tall, but originally it may have closely matched the height of the spire of the tower that replaced it in 1869.

Situated on a hill 10 km (6 miles) south of Ballycastle, with stunning views of the Antrim countryside, this early church was associated with Bishop Olcán, a 5th-century contemporary of St Patrick. The present Church of Ireland church, dedicated to St Patrick, was constructed in the mid-19th century. Prior to the completion of the bell-tower of this church in 1869, the Anglican community used the round tower as their belfry. The doorway faces south and almost gives the appearance of looking away from the nearby 19th-century church and is unusual for its tall and slender shape. To counteract any weakness such a tall opening may have presented, the builders placed a massive lintel, modestly embellished with an architrave, across the top of the doorframe, spreading the weight of the masonry above. Here we can also see small holes around the exterior of the tower, which reflect the scaffolding used by its builders.

ROUND TOWERS OF IRELAND

DRUMBO, CO. DOWN

Overlooking the Lagan valley, the patron saint of Drumbo was Mochuma, who was reputedly blessed by St Patrick while still in his mother's womb. A Presbyterian church has stood here since the 17th century, and in the adjoining graveyard are the remains of a round tower that today stands just 10 m (32½ ft) tall. The most obvious feature is the tall, slender doorway that faces east towards the present church. Within the interior, there are no rings of stone corbels or offsets to support the wooden floors. Instead, we see a series of large holes in the masonry that resemble sockets to secure floor joists, but it seems more likely that these were wooden corbels that supported the timber floors.

Drumbo round tower.

DRUMLANE, CO. CAVAN

Drumlane Church and round tower on the shores of Lough Derrybrick, Co. Cavan.

The church of Drumlane is associated with St Mogue (Maodhóg), better known today as Aidan. He was reputedly born on an island on Brackley Lough, near Bawnboy, Co. Cavan. As a young man, he went to Wales to receive training under St David, and on his return to Ireland established a monastery at Ferns, Co. Wexford. According to one medieval biography of the saint, he was a fellow pupil of St Molaise who later founded Devinish Island on Lough Erne. Though it appears that Mogue spent much of his career in Wexford and Wales, he was held in high regard by the community at Drumlane, and the church here treasured a 12th-century reliquary known as the Breac Maodhóg, now in the National Museum of Ireland.

The monastery was re-established as an Augustinian house in the 1140s and it became known as the priory of St Mary, but the round tower here was probably constructed a few decades previously. The tower stands a little over 11 m (36 ft) tall, and its elevated doorframe is embellished with a raised architrave, like at Kilree, Co. Kilkenny. The upper two-thirds of the tower is crudely constructed compared to the ashlar-block build of the lower section. On the northern side are two animal carvings, representing birds (one may possibly be a horse). Weathered and difficult to discern, there is no doubt that they were carved by the builders of the tower, but their early 12th-century symbolism is not known.

CLONES, CO. MONAGHAN

The town of Clones owes its origins to an ancient church founded here by St Tiernan (Tighearnach) (*d.* 550) who was reputed, at St Brigid's explicit request, to have been baptised at Kildare. The remains at Clones consist of a round tower, a 12th-century sarcophagus, a decorated high cross known as the Market Cross and a church dedicated to Saints Peter and Paul. The round tower is situated in a graveyard that represents the core of the original church. The tower stands 23 m (75 ft) tall and is almost complete, except for its roof. The narrow door of the tower faces east, probably in the direction of where a contemporary church formerly stood, but nothing survives today.

A high cross elaborately carved with Biblical scenes has stood for centuries in the Diamond, the old market square in the centre of Clones. This cross comprises the head and shaft of two different high crosses that probably once stood close to the round tower. Also in the town are the remains of a 12th-century church, sometimes known as the Abbey Church, which is believed to have been built around 1150 for the Augustinian Order of Canons Regular.

In the graveyard at Clones, close by the round tower, is a fine example of a stone shrine or sarcophagus carved into the shape of an early Irish church, possibly in the 12th century, to mark the grave of St Tighearnach. At one end are the faint remains of a figure wearing a mitre, probably representing St Tighearnach. The sarcophagus may be a stone copy of a metal shrine.

INISHKEEN, CO. MONAGHAN

Perhaps better known today as the birthplace of Monaghan's most famous poet, Patrick Kavanagh, Inishkeen was the site of an early monastery founded by Bishop Daigh (*d*. 588). Reputedly baptised and educated by Molaise of Devenish, Daigh was hailed as one of Ireland's finest craftsmen. The remains of the round tower stand just 13 m (42½ ft) tall and, apart from the large stone forming its sill, the elevated doorway appears to be largely rebuilt in more recent centuries. No trace of the medieval church survives and the former Church of Ireland church, now closed, was constructed in 1854.

Inishkeen round tower.

DEVENISH, CO. FERMANAGH

Devenish Island on Lower Lough Erne is another wonderful example of an early monastic foundation on an island that grew in importance over the centuries and became an important place of pilgrimage. Founded in the middle of the 6th century by St Molaise, who we are told was a fellow pupil of St Mogue (Maodhóg) of Drumlane. Among the many highlights is arguably the most perfect round tower in Ireland, and the interior is also one of the more accessible to visitors. It stands 25 m (82 ft) tall and is very well constructed with ashlar blocks of sandstone. The elevated doorway has an architrave around the frame, which we have seen elsewhere.

It is recorded that all the churches on Devenish Island were burned in 1157. Whether or not the round tower was a casualty is not clear, but it is interesting to note the foundations of a second, earlier tower a little to the north. It is certainly tempting to speculate that this older tower was severely damaged by the fire in 1157 and replaced by the one that we see today. The Romanesque features suggest that it was standing in 1176, when Domhnall, son of Mhlaoibh Ó Maoil Ruanaidh, king of the tribe Fir Mhanach, was murdered within by his own kinsmen. The circumstances are unclear, but it is worth noting that Domhnall as king might even have sponsored the construction of the tower.

Visitors can take a ferry from Trory Point, just outside Enniskillen, to reach the island.

At the top of the Devenish Island tower there is a cornice. This feature is common to many round towers, but this one is unique in its decorative frieze of four carved heads, one above each bell-floor window.

Devenish Island round tower, viewed from above. The circle of grass beside it represents the foundations of an earlier round tower, perhaps the one damaged by fire in 1157.